D1517214

DATE DUE			
APR 4 1982			

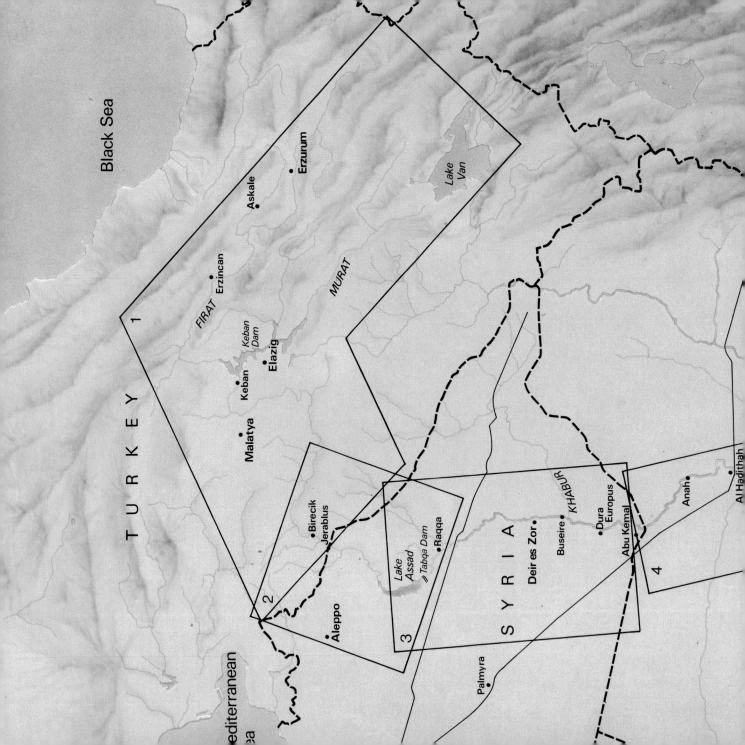

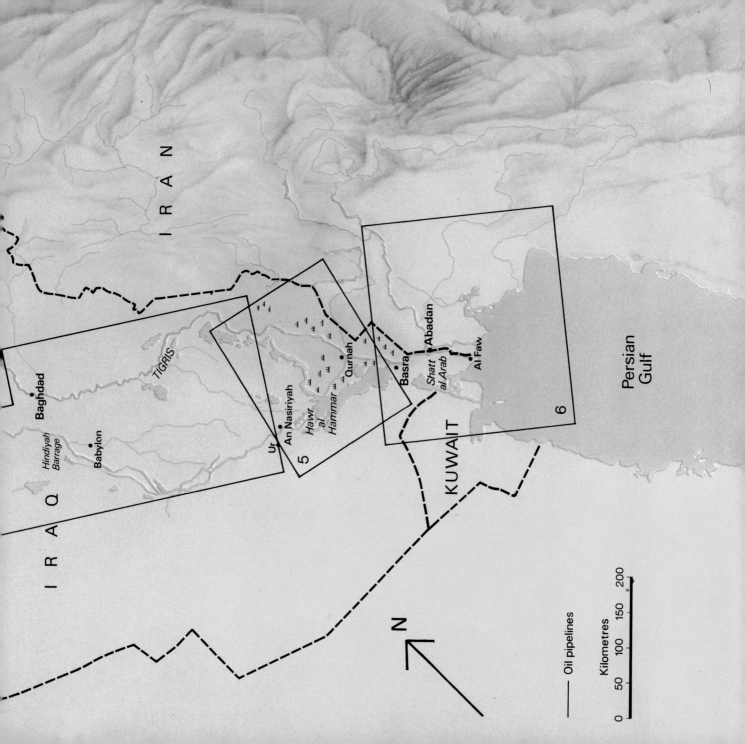

IRAN

IRAQ

Baghdad

Hindiyah
Barrage

Babylon

TIGRIS

An Nasiriyah

Ur

Hawr
al
Hammar

Qurnah

Basra

Abadan

Shatt
al Arab

Al Faw

KUWAIT

Persian
Gulf

5

6

N

—— Oil pipelines

Kilometres

0   50   100   150   200

The Euphrates

Rising high in the mountains of north-east Turkey, the Euphrates follows a long and winding course through Syria and Iraq until it reaches the Persian Gulf. The longest river in western Asia, the Euphrates shares much of its lower valley with the other great river of the Middle East – the Tigris. Together these streams have created a great and fertile region which is the true cradle of Western civilization. Today oil is the new wealth of the Middle East, but it is the waters of the Euphrates and its sister stream that have made it possible to inhabit, cultivate and conquer the vast desert lands.

In this book the authors take us on an unusual journey down an unusual river. We are shown not only the remains of the glittering worlds of the ancient past, but also see how the inhabitants of the countries through which the river passes have learnt to adapt to and control the whimsical moods of the great Euphrates.

John and Julie Batchelor are experienced travellers of some of the world's most unique places. They met in Turkey, and have journeyed together throughout the Middle East as well as to such distant shores as Indonesia and central west Africa. They have both studied and photographed the impact of modern civilization on the local peoples and environments they have encountered along the way. They are also the authors of *The Congo* in this series.

Biblical scene by the River Euphrates in Babylon.

The Euphrates

John and Julie Batchelor

Wayland/Silver Burdett

Rivers of the World

Amazon
Colorado
Congo
Danube
Ganges
Euphrates
Mekong
Mississippi
Nile
Rhine
Rio Grande
Seine
St Lawrence
Thames
Volga
Yellow River

First published in 1981 by
Wayland.Publishers Ltd
49 Lansdowne Place, Hove
East Sussex, BN3 1HF, England
ISBN 0 85340 806 8

Published in the United States by
Silver Burdett Company
Morristown, New Jersey
1981 printing
ISBN 0 382 06518 2

Phototypeset by Trident Graphics Limited, Reigate, Surrey, England

Printed in Italy by G. Canale & C.S.p.A., Turin

Contents

The source: Erzurum to Jerablus

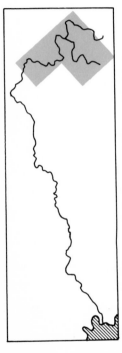

The Euphrates river rises in the rugged mountains of eastern Turkey, in the region known as Anatolia. It has two main source streams – the Murat and the Firat – and is in fact known in Turkey as the Firat river until it crosses the border into Syria.

The Murat river is the southernmost of these two streams, gathering water from the mountains to the northeast of Lake Van. Its remote source is near the village of Taskesan, at an altitude of about 2743 metres (9000 feet). The Firat, the main source, rises in the Kargapazari Mountain not far from the important town of Erzurum, then heads westwards before turning south towards its junction with the Murat river.

We begin our journey at Erzurum. Around the town, which is set in a valley, spread green fields irrigated by the waters of the river. But the bare, forbidding mountain slopes above us seem an unlikely spot for the source of a river which, as we will discover later, has brought fertility to desert regions and provided the raw materials for the start of civilization itself.

Right *The Murat, one of the Euphrates' source streams, rises in the mountains towering over Lake Van.*

Below *Green pastures nestle in a volcanic landscape in Turkey.*

Until about 10,000 BC this whole area was covered by ice, and it was not until the ice began to melt and retreat northwards that the river was formed and the first men started to appear in the hills. Recent excavations have revealed that settled communities probably lived in these mountains as long ago as 6500 BC. Eastern Anatolia may well be the place where agriculture, animal-rearing and religion were practised for the first time in man's history. This would have been possible because the country, all those thousands of years ago, would have looked very different from what we see today. The melting of the ice created conditions that produced huge forests, full of wild animals and plentiful supplies of water. Evidence has been found that the early inhabitants of the area traded throughout the Middle East in a commodity called obsidian, a very hard, volcanic rock resembling bottle-glass, which was useful for making tools. The mountains were formed through volcanic activity, and even today earthquakes occur quite often.

At this stage the Euphrates is too small to follow by boat, so we will take either the road or the railway. It is thus that we start on a journey which will take us over 2754 km (1600 miles) south from these bare mountains, through deserts and plains to the Persian Gulf.

As we leave Erzurum, the road and railway closely follow the course of the river. We soon

Left The town of Erzurum, which was an important centre during the Byzantine period.

Above *A Kurdistan woman wearing traditional embroidered clothes under her cloak.*

pass the airport on our right and a few kilometres further on the town of Llica, which has hot springs and a big new sugar factory for processing the sugar-beet grown in the nearby valleys. The climate on this high plateau is very harsh. In winter temperatures sometimes drop to −37°C (−34°F), and in summer often rise well above 40°C (104°F). No doubt the people of Llica are thankful for their hot springs during the hard winter.

Both the road and the railway leave the river for a while at Askale, threading their way through mountains before dropping down on to a lower plateau. As the river continues west we see many signs of the very long and violent history of the region. The route we are following is the main road from East to West – from Asia to Europe – along which trade has been carried on for thousands of years. It was also the route taken by the great invading armies from the East: from the Hittites to the Mongols and, in recent times, the Russians. From the south, too, came the Assyrian forces, followed centuries later by the great Moslem armies of the Middle Ages. The traffic has not all been one way, for many armies have marched in from the West, including the Greek troops of Alexander the Great, Roman armies, and many more. It can truly be said that Anatolia was in the past the crossroads between East and West, and that whoever controlled Anatolia also controlled the most important trade route. This is one of the reasons why the whole history of the region is one of battles, invasions and a sequence of civilizations which, if only briefly in some cases, have made Anatolia their home.

The next place we come to gives us an opportunity to examine the remains of one of the earliest civilizations. At Altintepe, in 1938, a tomb

Above *Assyrian chief with a captive prisoner and two men pleading for his release.*

was discovered which provided a great deal of information about the Urartian people who lived in this region in about 1000 BC. The artefacts which archaeologists brought out of this tomb – fine clothes, jewellery, gold and bronze objects, as well as inscriptions on stone slabs – show us that these people lived in a well-organized society with a king, noblemen and armies, and that they built fine palaces and had their own form of writing. This town was evidently the regional capital, and controlled the north-western section of the Urartian Empire, of which the main capital was further east near Lake Van. In 1200 BC the Urartians had conquered the Hittites, another advanced and well-ordered people who

Left One of the alleged sites of the Garden of Eden on the banks of the Euphrates near Elazig in central Turkey.

Above *Steam locomotives are still used to transport goods in Turkey.*

Left *Oxen draw a cartload of children across Lake Van.*

had controlled the area from about 2000 BC, but a thousand years later the Urartians were themselves defeated by the Medes.

If we go a few miles further west we come to the town of Erzincan, where we see an example of another great natural force which has played a part in forming the country. We will notice straightaway that the present town is relatively new. There has been a town on the site for thousands of years, but in 1939 the great power that shaped these mountains and still remains active, though bottled-up, broke out and in a devastating earthquake completely destroyed the old city of Erzincan. Marco Polo, the famous Italian traveller of the thirteenth century, passed this way and wrote about the weaving, wool and copper craftsmanship of the region. We will still see men working in copper in Erzincan today.

The road further west is too difficult to drive along for most of the way, so we must continue by train. The railway follows the Euphrates for another 112 km (70 miles) or so, until the river turns south and disappears into more wild mountains. The railway takes an easier route, making its way through striking mountain scenery to Elazig where we leave the train and go by road to see the Keban Dam.

The Euphrates has already travelled about 480 km (300 miles) from its source, all the time gaining more water and more power. Now, at Keban, we find man putting this power to work for the first time. Keban is at the spot where the major tributary, the Murat, joins the Firat: the united streams then plunge down together into a deep rock gorge. The building of the dam at Keban was the biggest civil engineering project undertaken by Turkey in the 1970s. It is a rock-filled dam, the top of the barrage measuring 1155 metres (3800 feet) across. The main purpose of the project is to produce hydro-electric

Right *Giant carvings have been hacked out of the rock on the wild slopes of Mount Nemrut.*

Above *A farmer and his family drive home from market in the evening light.*

power. The force of the water turns the turbines which produce electricity. Most of this electricity is taken by pylon over 965 km (600 miles) to Istanbul – the capital of Turkey – where it is used to power industries and factories.

The river still has a long distance to travel before it forces its way out of the mountains, so we still cannot follow its course by boat. Returning to the train, we rejoin the Euphrates at Birecik, where it breaks free at last from the mountains of Anatolia and approaches the border with Syria.

Left *The Euphrates passes through some spectacular scenery near the town of Elazig.*
Right *A mountain village girl bakes bread in a stone oven.*

The upper Euphrates to the Tabqa Dam

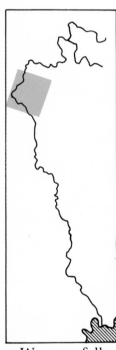

We cross into Syria at the frontier town of Jerablus, leaving the railway to continue its journey eastwards on the Turkish side of the border. The road heads off south-west to the city of Aleppo, but that is not the route we shall take, for we can at last get on to the river and move south. This is not without its difficulties, however, as there are many shallows and sandbanks in the river and it is impossible to use a boat of any size. We shall have to hire one of the local flat-bottomed boats, which look like large canoes.

We carefully make our way downstream, helped along by the strong current as we thread our way through the maze of islands. There is little sign of life along this stretch. The banks appear deserted and we see no fellow travellers on the river, just a great variety of bird-life everywhere. Later we pass signs of cultivation along the banks, but this is rare. Wheat, cotton and barley are grown with the help of water from the river, which is pumped up to the fields and circulated through irrigation channels.

The river is carrying huge quantities of silt which it has brought down from the mountains

Below *These beehive-shaped houses in Syria are built of mud.*

Bursting bales of cotton waiting to be taken to market.

of Anatolia. This provides a rich soil for farming, but it also makes life rather unpleasant when we try to land on the bank or on an island. We have to pick our spot very carefully, as there is no sand here, just thick gluey mud, and we may find ourselves sinking in up to our waists. Another strange thing we notice about the Euphrates is that it hisses all the time. The reason for this is not known, but it is thought that it may be escaping gas, produced by rotting vegetation trapped in the deep mud at the bottom of the river.

About 32 km (20 miles) further on, we make our first real contact with the outside world again when we come to Tell Ahmar. Here a ferry crosses the river, carrying people, animals and produce from one side to the other. It is an interesting spot, because it gives us an opportunity to take a close look at a 'tell'. Even in the short distance we have travelled since we crossed the border into Syria, we have already seen many of these strange mounds along the banks.

These flat-topped hills are, in fact, the sites of ancient settlements. A village was built on a particular spot and then, for some reason, abandoned – perhaps because of flooding or famine, or because the people were driven out by enemy forces. Then, years later, another village was built on the same spot and was, in turn, left to

Above *A mound of red peppers makes a colourful display.*

fall into ruins. This happened dozens of times and slowly the mound grew: at a rate, it is estimated, of about 12 cm (5 inches) every hundred years. This is very interesting for the archaeologists, as it means that when they dig down

Left *A craftsman in his workshop skilfully turns out pots.*

through a tell the whole history of the area is revealed to them. Through examining tells such as the one at Tell Ahmar, archaeologists now know that settlements have existed in this region for nearly 5000 years. Today an old fort crowns the top of Tell Ahmar, and if we climb to the top we may find pieces of broken pottery that are thousands of years old.

As we travel on, the river banks become busier. We see high cliffs bordering the river, many small villages, and dozens of little pumping stations which take the water of the Euphrates to the fields. There is very little rain in this area, only around 76–200 mm (3–8 inches) a year, so irrigation is essential for growing crops. The river banks are teeming with birds, mainly partridges and black terns. At certain times of the year we would also see vast flocks of migrating birds making their way south, following the river as we would follow a road.

A few kilometres further on we find the river beginning to broaden out, gradually at first, but then more and more until it becomes obvious that we are entering a lake. This is a man-made lake, produced when the Tabqa Dam was built in 1974. We must travel over 78 km (49 miles) along the lake before we come to the vast wall of the dam itself. An impressive sight, it is one of the largest earth dams in the world, stretching 4.3 km (nearly 3 miles) across the Euphrates

Left *These magnificent water-wheels harness the water's energy to produce power to drive machines.*

Above *The Tabqa Dam, which was built in 1974, provides water for irrigation and hydro-electric power.*

river valley. It is 29 metres (96 feet) high, has a base over 486 metres (1600 feet) thick, and during its building employed 13,000 workmen. The construction of the dam is certainly one of the most important developments in Syria for many years. It produces hydro-electric power which helps to run Syria's industries, and the lake has made it possible to irrigate and farm more than 606,000 hectares (1½ million acres) of land.

The Euphrates river has always provided water for cultivating crops, but in the past it only supplied a narrow strip of valley. At different times of the year, the river provided either too much or too little water, for its flow varies a great deal. In the spring, following the melting of the snows in the mountains, the river is about 6 metres (20 feet) deep and floods large areas on either bank, but by September the level has dropped to about 1 metre (3 feet). With the construction of the Tabqa Dam it is now possible to

Above *Passing the time of day in a village in Syria.*

control the flow of water and to store it in the lake for use all year round.

Because of the unpredictability of the water level, the Euphrates river has never been a major shipping route. In earlier times important caravan routes followed the river closely on their way north to Aleppo, but the merchants kept to their camels rather than risking the waterway. Today the transport routes still follow the river but are now, of course, roads and railways. The British have taken an interest in the Euphrates for centuries, as it formed a part of the major route to India and the Far East. One of the early Europeans to follow this route was Ralph Fitch, who in 1583 was sent as a messenger by Queen Elizabeth I of England to the Grand Mogul and Emperor of China.

Two hundred and fifty years later, when the British were urgently searching for a quick route to India, one of the possibilities they considered was building a canal from the Mediterranean coast of Syria to the Euphrates and then sailing south-east to the Persian Gulf. In 1835 Colonel Francis Rawdon Chesney was sent to the area to see if the idea was feasible. With him went a large group of men and two steamboats which were transported in sections. With some difficulty – and the assistance of 840 camels and 160 mules – he reached the Euphrates, assembled his boats and set off. As we have seen there are many shallows and sandbanks on the upper Euphrates, and the Colonel had a great deal of trouble in navigating the river, taking thirty-four days to travel 160 km (100 miles). He then started to make better progress but luck was not with his expedition. As the two boats – called *The Tigris* and *The Euphrates* – were sailing south, a storm blew up and *The Tigris* was hit by a freak tornado which sank the boat and drowned twenty-one men. *The Euphrates* did in fact make it to the Persian Gulf, becoming the first steamship ever to make the trip, but the British government – discouraged by the problems of the journey – lost interest in this route to India and turned their attention to other possibilities.

Right *Wandering Bedouin tribesmen drive their livestock across the Syrian desert.*

The middle Euphrates

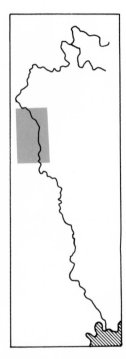

Soon after bypassing the dam, we find the river is crossed by a railway bridge. In recent years the railway has been extended up into the hills of the north-east in order to transport the produce of the agricultural area around El Haseke to the markets of Aleppo, Homs and the Syrian capital, Damascus. This region is known as the Jezire, and is called by some people the 'California of Syria' because of the rapid development over recent years of the growing of wheat, barley, cotton and rice. This area is now the country's main granary.

We pass the town of Raqqa on our left, and a little further on the waters of the Belikh river join those of the Euphrates. We are passing through a well-populated area with many villages along the river banks. Now that the Tabqa Dam is providing electricity and water for irrigation, this region is also developing and bringing a new prosperity to the farmers. Sheep and grain crops are the main products here.

The Euphrates is now a broad river, presenting us with few problems in our small boat. We pass a number of quite large islands, particularly on the long wide bends in the river. As we come round one of these bends about 24 km (15 miles)

Right *Harvesting wheat, one of Syria's most important crops.*
Below *Milking a flock of sheep.*

below Raqqa, we see another important factor in the economy of modern Syria. Here an oil pipeline crosses the river, carrying oil from the Karakok Mountains in the north-east out to the oil terminal at Baniyas on the Mediterranean coast.

The river's current is moving swiftly, and we make good progress. Along the banks we see flocks of birds, and catch glimpses of the railway line that follows higher ground on the left bank. The road follows the course of the river on the right bank. We also see many ruins dotted along the river, some dating from as far back as Roman times. In the first and second centuries AD the Euphrates formed the eastern frontier of the Roman Empire, and many of the ruins we pass are the remains of forts built by the Romans or their allies to protect and defend their frontiers. Occasionally we can see evidence of later occupations, by the Arabs and most recently by the Turks.

We soon reach the town of Deir es Zor, an important administrative centre and the point where the railway line parts company with the Euphrates and strikes out north-east to the Turkish border. Just south of the town is another important historical site, the castle of Qallaat Ali which overlooks the Plain of Siffin. This is the

Left *The Euphrates at Raqqa, where an oil pipe crosses the weir.*

Right *This road was built by the Romans in the days when their empire stretched as far as the Euphrates.*

site of a famous battle which took place in AD 657 between the armies of Mn'Awiyah ibn Abi Sufyan and Caliph Ali. The battle was over the question of who should succeed the prophet Mohammed, founder of the religion of Islam. The battle did not end in a military victory for either leader, but in an agreement to differ and to follow their own ways. This great split in the Islamic faith produced the two main sects of Islam, the Sunni and the Shi'ah Moslems. In some ways the split is similar to that in the Christian church between Roman Catholics and Protestants, who both hold very different ideas and beliefs. It was a very important event in Moslem history, and one which has a great deal of influence in Moslem countries even today.

The character of the river and the surrounding country is now changing. We have left behind the cliffs and hills of the upper river and are entering a wide, flat flood plain. The silt from the river, spread over the plain during flooding, provides a rich soil. Here we see citrus groves and fields of cotton as we follow the river south, weaving our way between islands covered in tamarisk bushes.

Only 19 km (12 miles) after leaving Deir es Zor, we come to the confluence of the Khabur

Above left *A donkey grazes peacefully near Deir es Zor.*

Left *An Islamic map showing the Kaaba at Mecca as the centre of the world.*

Right *The ruins at Palmyra silhouetted against the evening sky.*

Above *Palmyra was destroyed by the Roman Emperor Aurelian in AD 272.*

and Euphrates rivers. The Khabur is the most important tributary to join the Euphrates since the mountains of Anatolia. At this point, on the left bank, we can rest briefly at the small oasis town of Buseire. In times past this was an important stopping place on the caravan routes from the south and east. From here the caravans headed west into the desert, making for Palmyra and eventually Damascus.

A visit to Palmyra is well worthwhile. It is a fascinating spot, an oasis in the middle of the desert. In the third century AD it was a very important place, a city enriched by the caravan trade, and the centre of an empire ruled over by Queen Zenobia, one of the few women rulers of ancient times. She was famed for her beauty, intelligence and bravery, and even used to lead her troops into battle. But the end came for Queen Zenobia in AD 272, when she was defeated in battle by the Roman Emperor Aurelian, who destroyed the city, captured the queen and carried her off to Rome. Today we can still see something of the magnificence of the city, with its colonnaded streets and a vast temple, much of

Tower tombs at Palmyra where stone coffins were laid.

which is still standing. The temple, in the centre of a courtyard over 83 metres (272 yards) square, was dedicated to the sun god, Bel.

The tower tombs are one of the most interesting sights in Palmyra. There are more than one hundred and fifty of them — some standing four storeys high and filled with stone coffins each carved with the head of the person buried inside. Today, however, few of the heads are left for many were broken off and stolen by Europeans — for museums and their private collections — in the late nineteenth and early twentieth centuries. On a small hill above the city there is a seventeenth-century castle which was built during the Turkish occupation.

Left *A shepherd tends his flock on barren-looking grazing land.*

Below *This mosaic, which is nearly 5000 years old, shows Sumerian soldiers with their captives.*

Back on the river, we move quickly on through the pleasant green valley. One of the many historical sites along the way is the massive walled city of Dura-Europus, which was first established during the third century BC. It was a garrison town, strategically placed to protect the caravan routes from the south. These caravans, often numbering thousands of camels and carrying goods of great value, needed a great deal of protection. There were many nomadic Bedouin tribesmen in the area who made their living either by plundering the caravans or by demanding money to allow the merchants to pass unharmed.

A little further on we could make a brief detour to visit the ancient city of Mari, the artistic and commercial centre of the Sumerian Empire which flourished nearly 5000 years ago. Just south of Mari we come to the border town of Abu Kemal, where we see the modern-day caravans. Many brightly-painted trucks are parked in the main square, and there is a great bustle of activity as trucks are loaded and unloaded. Engines are repaired and everything is made ready for their journeys, either north to Aleppo in Syria or south by the ancient caravan route to Baghdad, capital of Iraq. Now we too must prepare ourselves for the next part of our journey when we shall cross the frontier, leaving Syria behind and entering Iraq.

Right *This beautiful building in Syria is used for storing grain.*

Iraq and the lower reaches

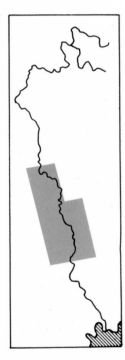

As we cross the border into Iraq, the valley of the Euphrates is narrow and barren. There is no sign of plant life or habitation, and the desert presses in almost to the water's edge. As we go on, however, we find ourselves once more following a thin fertile valley with limestone escarpments on either bank, and beyond them vast desert plains sloping gently towards the river. Iraq is mostly desert and arid plains, with the exception of a mountainous region in the north-east. The main features of the country are the Euphrates river and that other great river of the Middle East, the Tigris. So far, the Tigris has been following a course parallel to that of the Euphrates but much further to the east, after rising, like the Euphrates, in Anatolia in mountains close to the Keban Dam. Now these two great rivers come closer and closer together until they eventually form one huge fertile valley, the living heart of Iraq.

The journey from the border to this fertile plain is about 192 km (120 miles), and along the way we pass a number of ancient fortified towns which were originally built on islands in the

Below *A shepherd and his flock in the mountains of Iraq.*

The fertile plains of rural Iraq.

river. The largest is Anah, which we pass on the right bank. Long ago this town became too large for its island position, and has now spread out along the narrow river bank. All of the flat surrounding land is needed for housing and cultivation, and burying their dead has become a problem for the inhabitants of Anah. We may catch glimpses of caves hollowed out of the soft cliff face, providing burial chambers for these river people.

A few kilometres beyond Anah we are back in the modern world, at Al Hadithah where another oil pipeline crosses the river. Iraq is rich in oil reserves, and today the sale of this

Left *Oil refineries like this one have helped boost the economy of Iraq.*

Below *Traditional singing near the town of Ar Ramadi.*

commodity is the backbone of the country's economy. Oil is an increasingly valuable asset and a tremendous boon to those countries which possess it. In recent years oil has provided the money for the very rapid development that is taking place all over the Middle East. The saying that oil is 'black gold' has never been truer. From Al Hadithah, the pipeline snakes its way across the desert following the old caravan route to Palmyra, and then on to the oil terminal at Baniyas on the Mediterranean coast in Syria. The pipelines are the veins through which flow the lifeblood of the Iraqi economy: the oil flows out to the industrialized world, and money flows back in to pay for the development of the country.

At last we pass through 'the Gates', a cleft in the hills just above the town of Ar Ramadi, and enter the vast alluvial plain formed by the Tigris and Euphrates rivers. Before we can go any further we must first skirt the Ramadi Barrage. The barrage helps to prevent the Euphrates flooding, and also provides water for irrigation. Even though the surrounding land looks green and fertile, it is worth remembering that the average rainfall of the area is only about 200 mm (8 inches) per year. It is the river, and the river alone, which makes the valley's fertility possible. This whole region is laced with irrigation canals, channelling off the waters for use in the fields.

The Euphrates flows on in great loops for about 40 km (25 miles) until we reach the main road. If we want to travel to Baghdad, capital of

Above *Delicious fruits on display in a grocer's shop in Baghdad.*

Iraq, then we will take this road. Baghdad is only about 32 km (20 miles) to the west, and stands on the banks of the Tigris river. It would be a pity to come so far and not visit this city with its long and colourful history, so let's leave the river and pay a brief visit to Baghdad.

The city was founded in AD 762 by the Caliph Mansur, and became the centre of a vast Arab empire that extended from Spain to India. Its

Baghdad, the ancient centre of the Arab Empire, stands on the River Tigris.

Above *This man and his snooty camel seem quite at home among the modern blocks of flats in the background.*

Right *Baghdad's beautifully-decorated Kadimyah mosque.*

markets were famous for the exotic goods on sale from all over the world. Today the markets, or bazaars, are still fascinating places to visit, each craft occupying its own market or section of a market. There are markets for copper goods, cloth, carpets, leather goods, jewellery and almost anything you care to imagine. These markets are very much as they have been for hundreds of years. But Baghdad is not all old. It has its museums, palaces and old mosques, certainly, but it is also the bustling heart of a modern nation. Along Rashid Street, the main boulevard, are high-rise office blocks, hotels, shops and everything else you would expect to find in a modern capital city.

Above *The ziggurat at Aqar-Quf was built over 3300 years ago of mud bricks and reed matting.*

Below *A decorative horse built into the brickwork of the walls of Babylon.*

On our way back to the Euphrates we might stop off at Aqar-Quf, where we can step back over 3300 years in history to look at the ziggurat built by King Kurigalzu III. A ziggurat is a temple tower, and the core of this one is still standing, towering 51 metres (170 feet) above the surrounding landscape. It was built of mud bricks and reinforced by reed matting, obviously a system that was built to last.

Back on the river we quickly make our way downstream to visit one of the most famous sights of the area, the site of the city of Babylon. On the way we pass another barrage across the river, this time at Hindiyah, again used to control floodwater and irrigate the fields. About 32 km (20 miles) further on, a little to the east of the present course of the Euphrates river, we reach the site of ancient Babylon. Babylon was first mentioned in historical writings about 1750 BC, when King Hammurabi made it his capital. Hammurabi is famous for formulating one of the earliest known codes of laws, which were written down on clay tablets and some of which are still preserved today.

This period came to an end in about 1300 BC, when the Assyrians – the new power in the land – destroyed Hammurabi's city. The peak of Babylon's greatness came with the rebuilding of the city by Nebuchadnezzar, King of the Chaldees, around 602–562 BC. He built magnificent palaces and temples, but is best known for the wonderful hanging gardens, one of the famous seven wonders of the ancient world. The story goes that he built the gardens to please his wife, Amytas, who came from the green and fertile mountains of the east and missed the lush scenery of her homeland. There are, unfortunately, no signs of the gardens to be seen today.

After rejoining the busy river we pass on south through green fields and past many towns and villages. Much of the time, we seem to be higher than the fields around us. This is not an optical illusion, but rather an indication of how much

Right *This stone, carved with strange emblems, dates from the time of Nebuchadnezzar.*

Below *Monument to King Hammurabi of Babylon.*

Above *The high level of the river in some parts makes it liable to burst its banks.*

Below *Iraqi farmland provides plenty of work for local people.*

mud and silt the river carries with it. Over the centuries this mud and silt has been deposited along the banks until it has built up into an embankment enclosing the river and raising its level. The embankments, known as bunds, are artificially reinforced. Together with the barrages along the river, they are very important in controlling the spring floods, for if the river banks were to break all the land around would be severely flooded.

Before the river was brought under control flooding was quite common, and stories of great floods figure in many of the earliest writings from this area. It is thought by some historians that the Bible story of Noah's Ark and the Great Flood had its origins here. The Sumerians who lived in this region about 5000 years ago had a similar story – of a great flood and of one man being chosen by the gods to save mankind and the animals. There is some evidence for the story, for archaeologists have discovered very ancient pottery lying below a deep layer of silt, indicating that a great flood did occur and covered the land to a depth of about 8 metres (26 feet). Such a volume of water would certainly have flooded much of the Euphrates-Tigris plain. A German scientist, Werner Nutzel, has a theory that around 35,000 BC the world experienced a Warm Age, a temporary rise in the normal temperatures of that period which would, he calculates, have raised the level of the sea by about 5–6 metres (18–20 feet), and would certainly have caused widespread flooding in this area. If the theory is correct, then it would explain the Sumerians' flood story. But how did a similar story come to be in the Bible, which was written much later and by people living far away in Palestine? Well, the link might be the ancient city of Ur which we are just approaching.

Ur, or Ur of the Chaldees as it is often known, is a short distance away from the river a few kilometres south of the town of An Nasiriyah. The Sumerian Empire was made up of a collection of city states, each city having its own ruler. One of these city states was Ur, and excavations of this site have produced a wealth of information about life four or five thousand years ago. It was here that one of the earliest – possibly the first – forms of writing was invented. It is known

Above *A seventh-century clay tablet showing an outline map of the world.*

as cuneiform, from a Latin word meaning wedge-shaped, and consists of four kinds of wedge strokes made on clay. Putting the strokes together in different ways produced different meanings.

Above *Two awe-inspiring ruins of Ur: the ancient palace in the foreground, and in the background the ziggurat.*

But how does Ur come into the Bible flood story? The link is Abraham, one of the Patriarchs of the Old Testament, who lived in Ur until the city was overrun by invaders around 2010 BC. He then went to live in Palestine, and would almost certainly have taken the great Sumerian story of the flood with him, passing it down to his children who in turn would have passed it on to their children.

Today the most impressive sight still to be seen at Ur is the remains of a ziggurat, which stands 18 metres (60 feet) high. Only the first stage is left today, but originally it would have been rather like a pyramid consisting of three stages, each one smaller than the one below it. At the top there would have been a shrine to the god to whom it was dedicated. This particular ziggurat is built of mud bricks set in bitumen, a substance which occurs naturally at a spot near here where it can be seen bubbling up out of the ground. A ziggurat similar to the one at Ur is thought to be the origin of another Bible story, that of the Tower of Babel. Some historians think that this refers to a very big tower that used to stand in Babylon but has long since disappeared.

The royal cemetery of Ur has given us other interesting insights into life all those thousands of years ago. The kings were buried with all their wealth around them, everything from jewels to chariots. It is obvious from these objects that craftsmanship in Ur had already reached a high standard, and that many small industries must have flourished in this well-organized society. There is also evidence in the tombs that not only did the king take his wealth with him to the next world, but also his courtiers and guards. It seems that the people were happy to go with their king, who was also looked on as a god, for they do not seem to have died violently but rather to have taken a drug and gone quietly to their grave. Whatever the truth of the matter, we cannot linger here any longer but must get back to the river to continue our journey. We are about to explore an area quite different from any we have seen so far.

Right *Many beautifully-preserved works of art, such as this golden harp, have been recovered from Ur.*

The Marsh Arabs

The Euphrates now turns to the west and enters a vast region of lakes and marshes, a waterlogged area extending over some 15,500 sq km (6000 square miles). Here dwell a people who have developed a way of life perfectly suited to their strange environment. These are the Marsh Arabs, or Madan as they call themselves. With luck we will be able to find local guides to take us into the marshes.

We will make this part of the journey in a special canoe, called a *mashuf*, a long narrow boat with high prow and stern sections which help it to push a way through the reeds. We start in quite open water, with scattered reed beds dotted across the surface – the Hawr al Hammar is really a lake, and not the marsh proper. But soon the reeds close around us, and our boatmen sit at the front and rear using poles to push us through the strange green tunnel. Much of the time we can see nothing but the reeds, clouds of insects and the occasional bird flying overhead.

Suddenly we enter an open, sunlit lagoon. It is in the lagoons that the Madan build their homes on islands of reeds, homes which are also completely made of reeds. Apart from the house, there is just enough room on the island for the family's buffaloes. Reeds and buffaloes provide virtually everything necessary for life for the Marsh Arab. The reeds provide him not only with the materials for making his home but also with an income, as great bundles of reeds are collected to be sold for roofing throughout Iraq.

The shoots of the reeds are also the food for the water buffalo. These animals, it is thought, were first brought to the marshes by the Sumerians who imported them from India around 3000 BC. The buffaloes are very tame,

Right *Preparing reeds at Qurna. Reeds provide building material for houses, food for cattle, and are woven into mats which the Marsh Arabs sell.*

and lazy, and live with the Arabs almost as part of the family. They are rarely killed and eaten but are kept for their milk. Like desert Arabs, amongst whom it is traditional that only the men milk the camels, so here in the marshes we find that it is only the men who are allowed to milk the buffaloes. The milk is either drunk in its natural state or turned into yogurt. Not only does the buffalo provide milk, it also gives the Marsh Arabs fuel for their fires, for the dung is made into round flat cakes, dried and then burnt. There are very few trees in the marshes and therefore little possibility of making wood fires, so the buffalo dung is a very welcome alternative.

Once we come to a village we will certainly be invited to stay the night and join the people for a meal. The Islamic religion puts an obligation on its followers to entertain travellers and provide them with food and a place to stay. Every village will have its *mudhif* or visitors' house, and the size of the *mudhif* will indicate the wealth – or otherwise – of the village. The bigger the house, the richer the village. Some *mudhifs* are as big as churches and completely made of huge bundles of reeds. There we will be entertained with the very best the people can offer us, for they will feel that they have not been good hosts if they cannot put more food in front of us than we could possibly eat.

Left *Salting freshly-caught fish outside a Marsh Arab's hut.*

These Marsh Arab houses are built on little islands in the middle of lagoons.

Visitors may be entertained in this sturdy marshland house.

When we sit down on the floor to eat we will be joined by all the important men of the village, but the women will stay out of sight, for in a Moslem society women never eat with men. In the centre of the floor will be laid dozens of small dishes of rice, fish, mutton, birds and soup, as well as other things we probably will not recognize. On the ground in front of each person there will be a large piece of flat, unleavened bread, which looks rather like a sheet of brittle brown paper, but is in fact the 'plate'. We stretch out a hand – always the right one – take a handful of rice, and then some meat or fish, placing them on the bread and using our fingers to eat with. We must always remember to use only our right hand for eating, as food should never be touched with the left hand. This is because the Arabs consider that the left hand is the one which is used for unclean activities. Once we have eaten enough we finish off by eating the 'plate', so that nothing is wasted. There will still be a lot of food left over, which will be taken away for the women and children to eat. If there is anything left after that, it is fed to the animals outside. After thanking our generous hosts we set off again next morning, having spent the night sleeping on cushions on the floor of the *mudhif*.

As we go on our way, men carrying rifles and festooned in cartridge belts pass us in their canoes. They are on a hunting trip, possibly to shoot some of the many birds which live in these marshes, but more likely to hunt the wild boar. These ferocious animals are quite common here,

Above *This pair of storks have a bird's-eye view of the surrounding countryside.*

and provide dangerous and exciting hunting. We may also see fishermen at work. In recent years nets have been introduced into the area and these are now widely used, but the more traditional method is spear fishing. The fisherman stands in the bow of his boat holding aloft a spear with a five-pronged head, which he throws like a javelin as soon as he spots a fish below the surface.

Having progressed through the marshes we are nearing the end of our journey on the Euphrates river. At a place called Al Qurnah the Euphrates at last meets the Tigris river, and at this point the waters of these two rivers join to complete their journey to the sea by another name.

Journey's end: the Shatt Al Arab

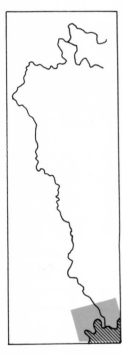

Al Qurnah is a pleasant palm-fringed town which stands at the very point where the Euphrates meets the Tigris. This strategic position enables it to control the route north to the capital, Baghdad, and has made it the scene of many battles over the last two or three hundred years. It is quiet enough today and has a developing tourist industry, partly because it is one of the many places that claim to be the site of the biblical Garden of Eden.

Here the Euphrates and Tigris rivers join and lose their separate identities, completing the last 185 km (115 miles) of their journey to the Persian Gulf under the name Shatt Al Arab.

The waterway is busy with small craft and the road follows the right bank. The border with Iran is now very close on our left. As we make our way down this last section of the river, we cannot help but notice another change in the character of the surrounding countryside. Gone are the fields of wheat, barley and vegetables so familiar along the banks of the Euphrates earlier. In fact we can hardly see a field at all, for we have now entered the biggest area of date palms in the world. As far as the eye can see there is

Right *Tending the dates, one of Iraq's most important exports.*

Below *One of the many date palm groves on the banks of the Shatt Al Arab.*

Above *Iraq is the leading date-growing country in the world.*

Left *A sixteenth-century impression of the dangers encountered by early traders.*

Right *Picturesque old houses in the busy trading centre of Basra.*

nothing but waving palm trees. It has been estimated that there are more than 18 million date palms in this area, and it is easy enough to believe that Iraq is the biggest exporter of dates in the world.

Our last port of call will be the town of Basra, a bustling modern city – the second largest in Iraq – with a population of around 750,000. It is the country's main port, and also has extensive oil-refining facilities to deal with the production

Modern ships load and unload their cargoes at the port of Basra.

from the nearby oil-fields, about 32 km (20 miles) west of the town. It is surrounded by date-palm plantations, and laced with irrigation canals. The presence of these canals has earned the town the title of 'the Venice of the East', but that is just about the only similarity to the Italian city of Venice.

Basra has been an important trading town and port for many hundreds of years. It was here that the produce of China, India and Africa came to be traded throughout the Middle East. The merchants of Syria, Turkey and Arabia used to assemble here to buy their goods, and also camels to make up the caravans in which they would journey home. Many would have followed the route we have taken along the Euphrates, making the hazardous trip to Aleppo, Palmyra or Damascus. After leaving Basra, a camel train would, with luck, take about seventy days to reach Aleppo.

Basra is still a busy trading town, but the character of the trade has changed. It is still the main entry point for all the goods that a modern nation needs, but the camels have gone and in their place are trains, trucks and boats ready to carry the goods to their inland destinations. Oil is the main business of Iraq today, but it is not exported through the port of Basra as the massive modern tankers cannot make the journey from the sea up the narrow Shatt Al Arab. We will see how that problem is overcome a little later.

Basra is not a place in which to spend the

Above *A floating oil-rig in the Persian Gulf, an area which produces about one-third of the world's oil.*

summer if you can possibly avoid it. Like most of Iraq, the temperatures at this time of year can rise to as high as 47°C (120°F). This great heat is much more uncomfortable to bear here because of the very high humidity, caused by the town's

59

closeness to the sea. It is a wet, sticky heat which feels much hotter than the dry heat of the desert, where there is little or no water and therefore no dampness in the air.

So let's move quickly on downriver. The border with Iran has now reached right down to the left bank, so we must keep to the right. We soon pass Iran's big oil-exporting port of Abadan and see the great refineries working away, another reminder of the importance of oil to these countries of the Middle East. On our bank, next to the road, is yet another sign of the presence of oil, Iraq's pipeline.

One hundred and twelve kilometres (70 miles) from Basra, we come at last to the Persian Gulf and the small port of Al Faw. As we stand on the headland, Iran is to our left and just a few miles to our right is Kuwait. Iraq has only a very small corridor of land giving it access to the Persian Gulf, and it is fitting that this entry to the outside world is provided by the waters of the Euphrates and Tigris rivers. Our journey is over, but we see that the oil still has quite a way to go. The pipeline leaves the headland and continues about 16 km (10 miles) out to sea to where an oil terminal has been built. Here the tankers take on their cargoes of oil without ever having to come into port.

Left *A sign of prosperity – oil burning fiercely at a refinery in Abadan, Iran.*

Kuwait is one of the important oil ports on the Persian Gulf.

We have followed the Euphrates river over 2574 km (1600 miles) from its source in the mountains of eastern Turkey to the Persian Gulf. We have travelled through lands rich in history and culture, and throughout our journey we have seen that it has been the river that has provided the basis for life. It has supplied the water for the irrigation systems that have made farming possible in areas which would otherwise be desert. The produce from the land enabled settled towns and villages to develop, and later the glittering civilizations which have prospered along its banks for over 5000 years. Today it does the same, and even more, for man has learnt how to harness the great power of the river to work for him, not only in providing water but also in providing electricity to power his new industries.

Today oil is the source of the new wealth of the region. But as we have seen, the oil is flowing out of the countries that own it and, unlike the waters of the river, that flow will not last for ever. For the present oil will give this part of the world the opportunity to regain some of the glories of the past, and to build new modern states. Whatever benefits oil may bring there is one thing we can be sure of, and that is that in another 5000 years' time the Euphrates river will still be flowing and will still be making a major contribution to the lives of the people who live along its banks.

Right *This supertanker symbolizes the Middle East's recently acquired wealth, but what will happen when the oil runs out?*

Glossary

Archaeologist   A person who studies the past by examining the remains of societies and cultures.

Artefact   Any object which has been made or shaped by man, such as a work of art, a tool, etc.

Assyrians   Ancient inhabitants of Assyria, a kingdom in northern Mesopotamia, whose empire stretched from Egypt to the Persian Gulf.

Barrage   A dam or other structure built across a river, especially one which increases the depth of water.

Bund   An Eastern word for a man-made ridge or bank built to confine the waters of a river.

Caravan   A group of travellers or traders, usually with a train of camels, passing through the desert.

City state   A political area consisting of a city and its surrounding region, of which the government is based in that city. In ancient times, both Athens and Rome were city states.

Cuneiform   The wedge-shaped characters used in the writing of several ancient languages of Mesopotamia and Persia.

Dam   A man-made barrier built across a river to control its flow.

Excavation   The methodical digging up of objects under the ground in order to discover information about the past.

Flood plain   A plain bordering a river, formed by deposits of sediment carried down by the river. If the river floods, the water spreads over the plain and more sediment is thus deposited, so that the level of the plain gradually rises.

Garrison   A force of soldiers which lives in and defends a town or fort.

Gorge   A small deep valley with very steep walls.

Granary   A region that produces a large amount of grain.

Hittites   Ancient inhabitants of Asia Minor (now called Anatolia), who built a great empire in northern Syria and Asia Minor from about 2000–1000 BC.

Hydro-electric power   Electricity produced by the energy of flowing water.

Mesopotamia   In ancient times, the name given to the region between the lower and middle reaches of the Euphrates and the Tigris rivers.

Mongols   Pastoral nomads from Mongolia in central Asia who, in the twelfth and thirteenth centuries AD, formed fierce armies and conquered a vast empire which included much of Asia and Russia.

Obsidian   A dark, glass-like rock formed when lava from a volcano cools and hardens very quickly.

Sandbank   A ridge of sand in a river, which is below the surface but may be exposed at periods of low water level.

Sediment   Any material carried and deposited by a river.

Silt An earth sediment which is finer than sand but coarser than clay.

Sugar-beet A plant which is cultivated for its white roots, from which sugar is obtained.

Sumerians Ancient inhabitants of Sumer, a civilization of city states in southern Mesopotamia which flourished between 4000 and 3000 BC.

Tell A large mound which results from the piling up of rubbish on a long-settled site.

Turbine A machine which is powered by the energy of a moving fluid such as water or steam.

Urartians Ancient inhabitants of the mountainous area around Lake Van in Turkey, who built a great empire in the ninth and tenth centuries BC.

Yogurt A thick custard-like food prepared by curdling milk by adding bacteria to it.

Ziggurat A temple tower or mound consisting of many layers, built in ancient Mesopotamia.

Further reading

Fichter, George *Iraq* (Franklin Watts, 1978).

Freya Stark & Fulvio Roiter *Turkey* (Thames & Hudson, 1971).

H. V. Geere *By Nile and Euphrates* (T. & T. Clark, Attic Press).

Gavin Young *Return to the Marshes* (Collins, 1977).

Gavin Young *Iraq: Land of Two Rivers* (Collins, 1980).

Hottam, David *Turkey* (Macdonald Countries, Silver Burdett, 1977).

Lady Anne Blunt *Bedouin Tribes of the Euphrates* (F. Cass, 1968).

Warren, Ruth *First Book of the Arab World* (Franklin Watts, 1963).

Facts and figures

Length of the Euphrates: 2735 km (1700 miles)
Length of the Tigris: 1850 km (1150 miles)
Length of the Shatt Al Arab: 859 km (535 miles)

ACKNOWLEDGEMENTS

British Museum 34 (right), 43 (both), 45; J. Allan Cash *frontispiece*, 10, 40, 44 (top); Documentation Arabe 36, 41 (right), 42 (both), 47, 53, 54, 56 (top), 57; Ian Griffiths 8, 11, 12, 14 (top), 16; Alan Hutchison 18, 19, 20, 21, 22, 24, 25, 29, 31, 32, 35, 38 (left), 59, 60, 61, 63; Iraqi Cultural Centre 55, 58; Iraqi Slides 38 (right), 39; Bruce Norman 49, 50; Popperfoto 14 (bottom); Sartec 44 (bottom); Spectrum Colour Library 23, 28, 30 (top), 46; John Topham Picture Library 17 (right), 26, 27, 37; Turkish Ministry of Tourism and Information 9, 15, 17 (left); Wayland Picture Library 13, 30 (bottom), 56 (bottom); Zefa *front cover*, 33, 34 (left), 41 (left), 51, 52.

Special thanks to the Hayward Art Group for the endpaper map.

Index

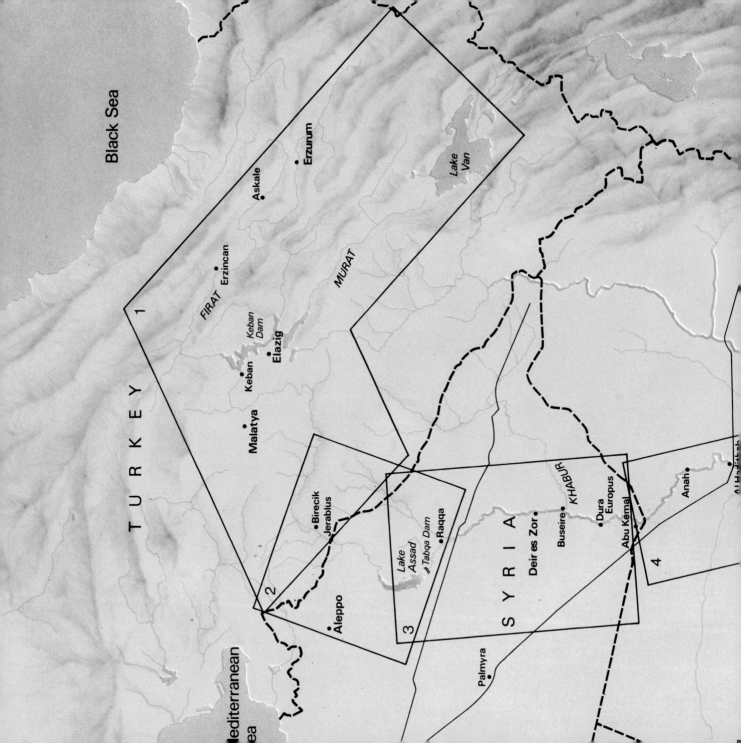

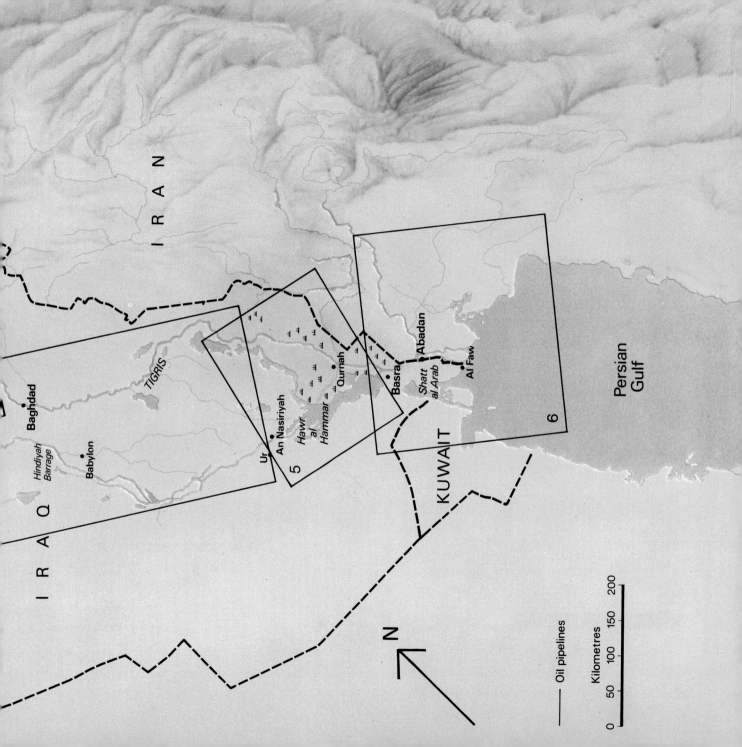

IRAN

Persian
Gulf

Abadan
Basra
Shatt
al Arab
Al Faw

KUWAIT

6

TIGRIS

Baghdad

Babylon

Hindiyah
Barrage

I R A Q

Ur
An Nasiriyah

Hawr
al
Hammar

Qurnah

5

N

Oil pipelines

Kilometres
0   50   100   150   200